D0646079

Dear Parent:
Your child's love of reading starts ...

Every child learns to read in a different way and at his or her own speed. Some go back and forth between reading levels and read favorite books again and again. Others read through each level in order. You can help your young reader improve and become more confident by encouraging his or her own interests and abilities. From books your child reads with you to the first books he or she reads alone, there are I Can Read Books for every stage of reading:

My First

SHARED READING
Basic language, word repetition, and whimsical illustrations, ideal for sharing with your emergent reader

1

BEGINNING READING
Short sentences, familiar words, and simple concepts for children eager to read on their own

2

READING WITH HELP
Engaging stories, longer sentences, and language play for developing readers

3

READING ALONE
Complex plots, challenging vocabulary, and high-interest topics for the independent reader

4

ADVANCED READING
Short paragraphs, chapters, and exciting themes for the perfect bridge to chapter books

I Can Read Books have introduced children to the joy of reading since 1957. Featuring award-winning authors and illustrators and a fabulous cast of beloved characters, I Can Read Books set the standard for beginning readers.

A lifetime of discovery begins with the magical words **"I Can Read!"**

Visit www.icanread.com for information on enriching your child's reading experience.

I Can Read Book® is a trademark of HarperCollins Publishers.

Alvin and the Chipmunks: Alvin and the Substitute Teacher
Alvin and the Chipmunks Motion Picture © 2013 Twentieth Century Fox Film Corporation and Regency Entertainment (USA), Inc. in the U.S. only. © 2013 Twentieth Century Fox Film Corporation and Monarchy Enterprises S.a.r.l. in all other territories.
Alvin and The Chipmunks, The Chipettes, and Characters TM & © 2013 Bagdasarian Productions, LLC. All rights reserved.
Printed in the United States of America. No part of this book may be used or reproduced in any manner whatsoever without written permission except in the case of brief quotations embodied in critical articles and reviews. For information address
HarperCollins Children's Books, a division of HarperCollins Publishers, 10 East 53rd Street, New York, NY 10022.
www.icanread.com

Library of Congress catalog card number: 2012956508
ISBN 978-0-06-225223-4
Typography by Rick Farley

13 14 15 16 17 LP/WOR 10 9 8 7 6 5 4 3 2 1
❖
First Edition

I Can Read!™
READING
2
WITH HELP
ALVIN
AND
THE CHIPMUNKS™
Alvin and the Substitute Teacher
By Jodi Huelin
Illustrated by Artful Doodlers
HARPER
An Imprint of HarperCollinsPublishers

Alvin loved music class.

It was his favorite school subject.

He looked forward to music all day.

Alvin liked it better than math.

He liked it better than lunch.

He even liked it better than recess.

Well, almost!

Alvin's teacher was Mrs. Melody.

"Mrs. Melody is the best!" Alvin said.

"She's the best!" seconded Simon.

"The best of the best!" agreed Theodore.

"What makes her so special?"

asked Dave.

Alvin thought Mrs. Melody

made learning fun.

A

"We have class outside on
nice days," Alvin said.
"Last week we played the steel drum
and the xylophone!" said Simon.

"For Mrs. Melody—an apple a day
keeps the doctor away," Dave said.
"Good idea," said Alvin.
"We don't want her to miss school."

In class that week, Alvin, Simon, and Theodore learned how to play brass instruments.

"Next week we'll start on woodwinds!" said Mrs. Melody.

"Cool!" said Alvin.

That Monday, the boys went to school.

"I'll try the clarinet," said Theodore.

"I'm thinking bagpipes," said Simon.

Alvin looked around.

Something was wrong.

Just then, Principal Wilson walked in.

"I have some bad news," she said.

"Mrs. Melody broke her leg.

She will be out all week.

Your substitute will be here soon."

"Substitute?" Simon asked.

"Substitutes are mean," said Theodore.

"They give double homework," said Alvin.

"This is terrible."

There was a knock at the door.

"May I come in?" said a voice.

Alvin put his head on his desk.

"Wake me when this day is over," he said.

Simon gasped.

Theodore laughed.

"What's so funny?" Alvin asked.

Then he looked up.

"Dave?" the boys said in union.

"My name is Mr. Seville," Dave said.

"I am your substitute teacher."

Alvin felt so lucky!

They would have fun in class,

just like they did at home.

Alvin acted goofy.

When Dave asked where pianos were invented, Alvin answered: "On the moon?"

Then it was time to sing.

Alvin asked if he could yodel.

He burped during scales.

"Do-re-mi-fa-BURP.

Ooops—sorry!" Alvin said.

Dave's face turned red.

Alvin's classmates giggled.

A

Soon the class began doing
whatever they wanted.
Some banged on the drums—loudly!
They weren't listening to Dave.
They were acting out.

Dave tried to take control.
"All right, guys, let's put down
the drumsticks," he said.
The class just ignored him.

"Can you teach us about opera?"
asked Simon.
"Or country music?" asked Theodore.
"Or go get ice cream!" said a boy.
"Ice cream! Ice cream!" the class yelled.

Alvin looked around.

Things were out of control.

"Dave looks upset," Alvin said.

"He looks sad," said Theodore.

Alvin wanted to help Dave.

So did Simon and Theodore.

But what could they do?

Just then the bell rang.

Class was over.

That night, Dave barely talked at dinner.
Then he was quiet at breakfast.
"You must be excited for Mrs. Melody
to return," he said before school.

Later, Alvin overheard Dave in the office.

Dave didn't see Alvin.

He was speaking with Principal Wilson.

"I'm a bad teacher," Dave said.

"The kids don't listen to me."

"Uh-oh!" Alvin said to himself.

Alvin felt terrible.

Dave wanted to be a great teacher.

But the kids weren't listening

and it was Alvin's fault.

He ran and got his brothers.

They rounded up the class at lunch.

"Starting today, we listen!" Alvin said.

"We learn!" Theodore said.

"What do you say?" Simon asked.

Their classmates agreed.
They didn't mean to be rude.
They didn't like making Dave
feel bad or upset.

Dave got to class late.

He expected chaos.

He expected a rowdy celebration—

a celebration he wasn't invited to!

Instead, he saw smiles.

Kids were sitting in their seats.

They were ready to learn.

"Who wants to learn about the history

of rock and roll?" Dave asked.

"We do!" the class said together.